EVERLASTINGS

PHOTOGRAPHY
BY
LAURA
EDWARDS

EVERLASTINGS

BEX PARTRIDGE

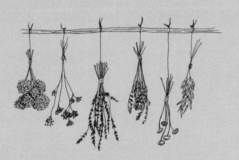

HOW TO GROW, HARVEST & CREATE
WITH DRIED FLOWERS

Hardie Grant

BOOKS

CONTENTS

WELCOME

INTRODUCTION

My journey with dried flowers began after a chance encounter. A fresh bunch given to me by a friend sat forgotten in a vase during a stressful time in my life. When I rediscovered it a few weeks later, the flowers, now dried, had become exquisite – their details amplified and their colours softened. Rather than throwing them out I organised them into a wreath, the first I ever made. That wreath hung on my kitchen wall for many years and marked the conception of Botanical Tales. I began to experiment, and as I did my confidence and creativity grew; I rediscovered pressing flowers and filled my workspace drawers with bundles of dried foraged flowers, seed heads and grasses.

I've learnt a lot. I once hung dried flowers from the wall of our old conservatory – I knew nothing about storage back then, and I was excited by this beautiful wall of flowers. But light and heat are just the wrong conditions, so when I sat down to make some wreaths, I found that the sunlight had scorched the bunches – not only had they lost much of their vibrancy but their petals had become so fragile they were impossible to work with. I was devastated, but I'll share what I learned from my mistakes.

I soon began to experiment with growing my own flowers for drying. I have always had a love of gardening – inherited from my *oma* and mother who were both accomplished gardeners. I've been the proud, frustrated owner of an allotment for over ten years and have been gardening for many more. After much negotiating with my husband, we agreed to turn over one third of our plot to flowers, and it's now filled with strawflowers as well as bee-and-butterfly-loving flowers for biodiversity.

I've seen a real shift in people's attitudes towards dried flowers over the years. When I first started sharing my work through social media, at fairs, and through stockists, I often heard that dried flowers evoked memories of grandmas' houses, where dusty old displays sat in fireplaces. It was lovely to hear how flowers can hold such strong associations, but, on the other hand, it was instructive hearing the negative connotations. People's perceptions about dried flowers is changing. Brides are choosing dried flowers over fresh as they can be kept as keepsakes, and more and more businesses are requesting everlasting installations and displays to show that their sustainability values are as important as their style. Then there are those of us that love them simply for their delicate beauty and their ability to keep us connected to nature and the seasons. It warms my heart to see dried flowers taking centre stage in so many people's lives and homes.

SETTING

THE SCENE

From Egyptian to Victorian times dried flowers were used for ceremonial purposes, crafting material and fashion. But in the 1980s, as cheap flowers from overseas became widely available, the popularity of dried flowers waned. The Egyptians, Victorians and everyone in between had no choice but to preserve flowers and herbs – they didn't have access to roses in every season or fresh herbs in the middle of winter. This constant availability is relatively recent, and I believe has resulted in dried flowers being pushed aside in favour of cheap, cheerful supermarket blooms.

Drying flowers and foliage is similar to preserving food. It's using summer bounty to take us through winter. A few boxes of dried flowers can bring joy to a dark winter's day, filling your home with the textures and tones of seasons past.

In part, the increased interest in dried flowers and foliage has come about with the rise of sustainability on people's agendas, with many of us far more aware of the impact our actions have on the world. The rise in the conscious craft movement has been well documented, and continues to grow as people choose to buy local, as well as considering the origins of their purchases. More and more of us are rejecting throwaway culture in favour of a slower pace and a more considered buying philosophy.

The same has been happening in the world of florists and flower growers. Using materials such as floral foam has become as stigmatised as smoking, and local growers of flowers are experiencing a resurgence. It's plain that a new attitude has arrived; one with a greater appreciation of, and gratitude for, the natural world.

WHY DRIED

FLOWERS?

I believe something magical happens to flowers when they're dried. Their vibrancy is dulled slightly, but their beauty is magnified. This beauty draws you in to intimately inspect a crinkle on a petal or a colour gradient you may not have noticed before. They have an understated beauty that rivals their blousy, extroverted former selves. They encourage you to slow down and observe their intricacies – one of the many reasons I enjoy working with them. Whenever I do events or markets, people are fascinated by dried flowers, almost in awe of their natural state, and this spans all ages and cultures. I've made wreaths for a Portuguese girl's bedroom walls and created mini-bouquets for Korean men to give to their mothers.

Dried flowers offer value as well as subtle beauty. Ever since Botanical Tales was born I've had sustainability at the heart of the brand and in many ways it's what has fed my love for dried flowers. I was already making more conscientious choices when it came to food and products, and this carried over to my choices of flowers and plants. Now I buy fresh flowers from local growers and dried flowers from UK suppliers as much as possible. I would encourage you to do the same, to work with what's available seasonally and support those who grow

in your own area. Growing and foraging makes up the rest of my dried flower needs.

I'm painstaking when building installations with dried flowers. I carefully reuse intact stems, and when I'm making commissions I save flower heads that break off in the process to use for other projects.

Two good tips:
- Keep a box of loose dried flower heads in your cupboard for decorating dining tables with when you have guests
- Keep loose sprigs of foliage to decorate gifts

In many ways I believe you'll find dried flowers offer a more sustainable option. Shop-bought flowers may have been flown many miles and grown using pesticides to be sold for a few pounds in your local supermarket. Dried flowers don't wilt; you can take your time creating with them, and for many months will look as good as new.

In the seasons when our gardens are filled with fresh flowers, dried may take a back seat, but it's in the darker days of autumn (fall) and winter that they come into their own. There's such pleasure in harvesting and drying your own summer blooms to create long-lasting displays of nature in your home.

HOW TO USE

THIS BOOK

The contents of this book is accessible to all, whether you're a seasoned gardener or a city dweller with no outdoor space, a florist or a creative soul. It's written in the hope of breathing fresh life into the world of dried flowers, bringing a modern touch to a traditional subject and providing all the information you'll need to dive into the world of everlastings.

By trial and error I've learned what grows and dries well, and I'll show my approach to gardening and harvesting with drying flowers in mind. Part of the beauty of growing and drying flowers is that everything is an experiment. My advice when drying material is always to give it a try; the worst that can happen is it won't work. I promise that mostly, you'll be pleasantly surprised.

The second half of the book moves on to how-to projects and inspirational ideas to help you get started on your own dried flower creations. I'm not a trained florist, rather an artist whose medium is flowers, so these projects have been created using methods I've developed, which may not follow floristry rules. While there's a structure to the projects and how-to guides, it's there to provide you with assistance rather than for it to be followed to the letter. Your style and preferences in colour and form may differ from mine and that is a good thing – I urge you to listen to your creativity and select materials that make your heart sing. You will create something entirely joyful if you take your own path rather than following exact, prescribed guidance.

There's no need to rush out and buy all the tools I recommend or to invest in bunches of dried flowers to work with – you can start with what you have to hand and play around to get used to working with dried flowers. Use up old bits of twine to make a wreath or repurpose a forgotten hair comb into a new dried flower accessory. Start to understand the care that needs to be taken when creating with dried flowers before investing in new tools and materials.

My hope is that this book is one you'll keep coming back to for inspiration. Of course the end result is the main reason for creating, but the beauty is really in the process itself. I lose myself in the making of a wreath or the pressing of flowers and find it's a calming, meditative way to spend a few hours. Try to embrace this side of the creating – enjoying the route to the end result as much as the finished project.

TOOLS

& MATERIALS

There are a few items I can't do without, none of which cost the earth, and some you'll probably have already. For the majority of my projects I work with natural materials wherever possible, which means I avoid glue guns and floral foam – not just for environmental reasons, but also because I enjoy the process of a more considered make.

1 *Raffia* – It gets a bad rap, but raffia is a favourite of mine. For my smaller wreaths I use it to bind flowers to the base and also to tie up flowers when I'm hanging them out to dry.

2 *Secateurs* – I have so many pairs of these! Apart from my usual garden secateurs I always have at least two pairs of portable, fold-out secateurs, one in my coat pocket and one in the car.

3 *Washi tape* – Use this to create pressed flower pictures as well as to hang them from the wall.

4 *Frog pin (pin holder)* – Really useful for holding dried flowers and foliage in place when creating displays in vases and under glass domes.

5 *Twine/twool* – Perfect for finishing off the ends of boutonnières or wreaths.

6 *Bullion wire* – Super-fine with a gentle kink running through it, I love using this wire for hanging florals and for some of my more delicate makes such as hair combs.

7 *Chicken wire* – For bigger displays, this can be used to fill the void of a big urn or vase and holding stems in place.

8 *Rustic wire* – A strong wire wrapped with raffia or natural twine that makes a brilliant base for floral crowns.

9 *Natural materials and ribbons* – I love the flow of a beautiful naturally dyed materials (such as in the background here) and ribbons, and use them to decorate most of my makes.

10 *Small, strong scissors* – I use these for snipping lengths or heads of blooms. Really useful for more intricate pieces and also good for when pressing delicate flowers with teeny-tiny stems.

11 *Wreath wire* – Relatively fine but durable wire that I use for larger wreaths, or if I'm making a wreath with a metal base and need a little more structure. I love the copper and brass-effect ones.

TAKING CARE

The main benefit of dried flowers is that they can last for years with a little bit of love and care. I have wreaths from the early days of Botanical Tales hanging on my wall looking as good now as they did three years ago.

If you follow these basic rules you should get many years of enjoyment out of your everlastings:

Sunlight – Avoid it if you can. Sunlight can and will bleach blooms rapidly, so hang wreaths or pressed-flower pictures in a place that doesn't get hours of direct sunlight. If you have no alternative space or it's perfect hung where the light falls, go ahead, but be prepared for the flowers to soften.

Moisture – Store and dry flowers in an area that's free from moisture. Your bathroom wall isn't the best place for a dried flower display and the same applies when storing materials. I had a disastrous year when I stored my dried flowers in our loft over winter. When I opened the hatch to retrieve them I discovered the space was full of damp air as a result of us rendering our walls the previous summer – I lost all my stock.

High heat – Although flower farms in the Netherlands dry flowers *en masse* using heated rooms for a short period of time to speed up the drying process, it can make the stems of flowers brittle and challenging to work with when drying at home. I always try to store my materials at, or below, room temperature and to avoid a boiling hot loft in the height of summer.

Looking good – To avoid displays that stir memories of your great aunt's faded bunches gathering dust in hidden corners, you'll need to give them a little bit of attention. I discovered the easiest way to keep displays dust- and cobweb-free is to blow them gently with a hairdryer on the lowest and coldest setting.

Freshening up – Flowers deteriorate at different rates, so I often have a play-around with a display, removing stems that are looking past their best and replacing them with new ones. I also take apart displays and change the style or flow for a fresh look, introducing a few new bits of material to update them. This is a great option when moving through the seasons, perhaps swapping pinks for orange tones as autumn (fall) arrives.

GROW

DIGGING

THE
FOUNDATIONS

When I first started working with dried flowers I had already turned a third of my plot over to growing them, and at that point I honestly believed that I could grow enough in that small space to start selling my own dried flowers. I quickly learnt that that wasn't going to be possible. Dried flowers shrink by at least a third of their former in-bloom size, so a lot of space is needed to grow and dry on a large scale. One season might yield two bunches of mixed everlastings in my growing space, which will make four wreaths if I'm sparing. I still grow though, because I'm a gardener at heart and enjoy it. A gift created using flowers I have grown from seed means so much more to me and the receiver. There is something deeply satisfying about taking a green shoot from a seed through its full life journey; nurturing it, caring for it then immortalising the bloom in a creation. In my back garden, which is relatively small, I can be incredibly productive and not leave an inch unplanted. I grow rows of strawflowers in a tiny strip of flower bed down the side of my house and wildflowers in front of my studio where stately teasels shoot towards the sky to be used during the winter months for indoor displays. I fill hanging baskets with pansies and violas and hang them from the branches of my quince tree, to be used for pressing throughout the summer, and poppy and scabious heads are left to go to seed to be dried later in the year, so I can enjoy their flowers in situ during the summer months.

When growing for drying, no matter the size of your garden or growing space, you'll need to think about the look of your garden year-round. You'll want to be able to enjoy the space, and as most dried flowers need to be picked just before they're at their best, I always intersperse them with flowers that I grow for pure joy rather than drying. This will ensure your space doesn't look depleted when the time comes to harvest your flowers. Also try to have in mind what your intentions are for the flowers once they're dried. If you primarily want to make wreaths, your flower choices will be quite different from what they will be if you wish to create big structural dried flower displays. And don't only think of the flowers you want to dry, consider leaves for pressing such as ferns and acers as well as seed heads and grasses to add textures to your displays. Seed heads and grasses also last for much of autumn (fall) and into the winter, ensuring your garden has year round interest and in many cases can be left to dry in situ saving time, space and effort.

My garden and allotment have a mixture of perennials and annuals, with a select few bi-annuals, such as honesty, which I couldn't be without. I have a greenhouse with an electric heater that gives me the ability to sow annuals from seed as early as January, giving me at least two crops of flowers such as helicrysums. Even if you don't have the luxury of a greenhouse, seedlings can be sown on a warm window sill and potted on in a sheltered spot on a patio.

Growing from seed doesn't need to be expensive either – ask friends with gardens for seeds at summer's end. Sign up to seed-swapping clubs online or start your own. The boom in garden centres is relatively new – my grandma tells me she created her beautiful garden by frequently swapping cuttings and seeds with friends and slowly building it up. If you buy packets of seeds, there's no need to sow a whole packet at once – I've made this mistake and it's always left me a ton of seedlings that I can't bear to throw away and struggle to palm off to

anyone. Just sow a sprinkling and save the rest for the following year, or swap some with a friend.

When it comes to the availability of specialist dried-flower seeds, we're now spoilt for choice. There are beautiful everlasting seeds coming to market now – I always choose a few interesting new options to try to grow and dry each year. Most good seed-suppliers will have a dried flower listings section, but remember that many blooms that aren't classified for drying do dry well when you use methods such as pressing and silica-drying (pages 45 and 48). Also consider buying flowers just for their seed heads; a combination of grasses, seed heads and flowers will see your garden through summer and autumn beautifully.

If your space is limited – a balcony or a shared outside area – it's still possible to grow and harvest a handful of flowers to dry. Good choices would be flowers such as zinnias, marigolds and pansies. Think about flowers that benefit from having their blooms picked – cut-and-come-again heroes such as violas – it'll give you greater longevity.

Here is a list of my favourite flowers to grow in the garden:

Annuals
- Cornflowers
- Nigella
- Pansies and violas
- Scabious
- Strawflowers
- Zinnias

Perennials
- Burpleurum
- Globe thistle
- Chinese Lantern
- Eryngium
- Monkshood

WHAT TO DRY

I could fill pages and pages with the details of all the plants and flowers that can be grown to dry. So I've kept it down to those that I enjoy and I use the most and that are among the most common to forage, grow or buy. I've separated the information into flowers, seed heads, grasses and leaves from trees. Remember that the possibilities are endless for drying, so even if I haven't mentioned the material here, you should still have a go.

As a general rule, the best plant material to dry tends to have slightly woodier stems that are less juicy in feel – think delphiniums rather than dandelions.

FLOWER	TIME TO PICK	DRYING METHOD
Alchemilla mollis (lady's mantle)	• Cut leaves throughout summer • Cut flowers when only the top buds are open	Hang flowers to dry and press leaves to preserve
Amaranthus caudatus (love-lies-bleeding)	• Cut at the base of the stem when flowers are just out before going to seed • Prop up when growing to keep off the dirt and mud	Hang dry
Ammobium alatum (winged everlastings)	• Cut when the topmost flower is fully open and the yellow centre showing	Hang dry
Astrantia (masterworts)	• Prolong cutting to avoid the flowers drooping when being dried	Hang dry and press
Catananche (cupid's dart)	• Prolong cutting to avoid the flowers closing up when being dried • Throughout summer, cutting encourages growth	Hang dry

FLOWER	TIME TO PICK	DRYING METHOD
Chamaemelum nobile (chamomile)	• End of the summer when flowers are in full flush, leave the leaves on for pretty dried foliage	Hang dry
Daucus carota (wild carrot)	• Cut full plant (not in the wild) to dry flower heads and seed heads together	Hang dry
Delphinium	• Cut at the base of the stem when half the flowers from the bottom up are in bloom	Hang dry and press individual heads
Echinops (globe thistle)	• Cut when the flowers have just appeared, leaving it too late will cause the flowers to go to seed	Hang dry
Gomphrena (globe amaranth)	• Cut when flowers are fully out	Hang dry
Gypsophila (baby's breath)	• Cut from the base of the stem when most of the tiny flowers are fully out	Hang dry or evaporation
Helianthus (sunflowers)	• Later in the summer when the petals are beginning to dry – not too fleshy	Lay flat to dry to ensure petals stay open
Helichrysums (strawflowers)	• Throughout the summer, cut for more growth, buds dry as well as main flowers, beware of flowers going over as they continue to develop whilst drying	Hang dry
Helichrysum italicum (curry plant)	• Once flowers are opened or nearly fully opened – buds can also look beautiful	Hang dry
Helipterum (paper daisies)	• Cut from the base of the stem when flowers are fully out	Hang dry
Hydrangea	• Cut the heads at the base of the stem, strip leaves, when the flowers are just beginning to turn. Picking them too early will result in droopy heads	Evaporation method
Limonium sinuatum (statice)	• Cut when flowers are fully out, leaving stem wings intact	Hang dry or evaporation method
Nigella (love-in-a-mist)	• Cut when the flowers are just out from the base of the plant, gather in bunches and leave most of the leaves in place	Hang dry
Tanacetum parthenium (feverfew)	• Middle of summer when flowers are in full flush, cut to encourage a second flush	Hang dry
Zinnias	• Cut and come again, pick when the flower is in full bloom	Lay flat to dry, or hang for a curled-up appearance

SEEDS	TIME TO PICK	DRYING METHOD
Allium	• Cut from the base of the stem once seed heads have formed	Hang or stand to dry
Clematis	• Cut when seed heads have just formed – don't leave too long or the seeds will disperse	Hang or string to dry
Cotinus coggygria (smoke tree)	• Cut the bunches of seed heads when the flowers have dispersed, cutting too early will leave you with wilted seed heads	Hang dry
Digitalis (foxglove)	• Cut the long spires when the seed heads are still green	Hang dry
Dipsacus fullonum (teasel)	• Cut the heads with a long stem just as the seed heads turn brown	Hang or stand to dry
Filipendula ulmaria (meadowsweet)	• Cut when the seed head is green	Hang dry
Linum lewisii (flax)	• Cut from the base of the stem when the seed heads have turned brown	Hang dry
Lunaria (honesty)	• Cut from the base of the stem when either the seed heads are green/brown (if they risk getting damaged by wind) or wait till they have turned a shimmery silver	Hang dry if picking when green, otherwise use straight away
Nigella (love-in-a-mist)	• Cut in bunches from the base of the plant	Hang dry but beware of seeds falling from open seed pods
Papaver (poppy)	• Cut from the base of the stem when seed heads have turned brown	Hang dry
Physalis alkekengi (chinese lantern)	• Cut when most of the seed heads have turned bright orange	Hang or string to dry
Scabious (pin cushion)	• Cut when the seed heads are green, before they turn brown and start to disperse • Stellata variety produces beautiful seed heads	Hang dry
Silene vulgaris (bladder campion)	• Cut from the base of the stem when seed heads have formed	Hang dry
Typha latifolia (bulrush)	• Cut before the seed heads start to burst, when they are still fleshy brown	Hang or stand to dry

GRASS	TIME TO PICK	DRYING METHOD
Avena sativa (oat)	• Pick later when golden	Hang dry
Briza media (quaking grass)	• Cut big bunches from the base when the seed heads have turned from green to brown	Hang dry
Cortaderia (pampas)	• Cut long lengths when the fluffy heads are out, beware of seeds dropping	Stems will be dry so use immediately or leave to stand in a cool place
Festuca (fescue)	• Cut from base when turned soft gold	Hang dry
Lagurus ovatus (bunny's tail)	• Cut from the base of the stem when the seed heads have turned golden	Hang dry
Phalaris canariensis (canary grass)	• Cut big bunches when the seed heads are still green	Hang dry
Phleum pratense (timothy)	• Cut big bunches from the base when the seed heads have turned from green to brown	Hang dry
Triticum aestivum (common wheat)	• Cut at the base when the seed heads have turned golden	Hang dry

LEAVES	TIME TO PICK	DRYING METHOD
Eucalpytus	• Cut when the leaves are no longer fleshy and have a sturdy structure to them	Use immediately in displays, the leaves will dry in the displays
Fagus sylvatica (beech)	• Pick leaves later in the season when they still have their colour, or wait until they turn and curl on the branch	Press or use the branches for displays as they are
Ferns	• Cut when the leaves are no longer fleshy and have a sturdy structure to them	Press
Pteridium (bracken)	• Cut from the base of the full leaf when all the leaf is brown	Use immediately or press gently to encourage them to flatten
Quercus robur (oak)	• Cut branches with leaves on before they start to leave the tree	Press
Salvia officinalis (sage)	• Cut a large bunch from the base later in the season when the leaves are less fleshy	Hang dry

HARVEST

BRINGING

NATURE HOME

Foraging isn't just for those who live in the countryside or near woods; city dwellers can find ways to source blooms, leaves and flowers with a little bit of creative thinking.

FORAGING IN THE WILD

Plant materials for drying can be found all around us, but some of the easiest places are woodland areas, roadside verges and natural grass or wild flower fields. I keep a pocket notebook to make lists of my favourite foraging spots such as the larch tree in my local woods which produces heaving branches of fir cones in December, or the nearby, unmanaged verges where oxeye daisies and wild carrot grow in abundance.

Once your eyes are opened to foraging in the wild, it's impossible to miss opportunities all around you. Driving down country lanes is a distracting business for me – I have to fight the urge to stop the car and jump

out when I spy the plump red seed heads of rosehips. In autumn (fall) I can't resist the browning leaves of bracken, filling my arms and the boot of my car every time we go out for a walk! Fir cones and twisted, gnarly branches can easily be found lying on the ground – perfect for making seasonal displays.

Wherever you end up foraging, make sure you're considerate – if you're unsure whether a plant is endangered or protected, leave it and return once you've found out. Never strip a plant completely of its leaves or seed heads – a few sprigs and branches here or there won't damage it, but any more and you risk stressing it and affecting future growth. It goes without saying you should never rip up an entire plant of course – the roots should always stay in the ground.

Places to avoid foraging (because at worst it's illegal and at best severely frowned upon) are public spaces such as maintained parks and conservation areas (these are becoming more common in urban areas as a way to protect the small but important green space cities have). And do take care when foraging from road verges – it's all too easy to put your life in danger on the edge of a road trying to get that one perfect cow parsley seed head. It's also worth bearing in mind that any material foraged close to roads will probably be covered in dust and pollution, so choose wisely.

Take care when taking cuttings from trees or bushes – while it can be tempting to rip a branch from its trunk when you see a perfect collection of leaves, it's very damaging. I always carry a fold-away pair of secateurs (page 17) with me to make the necessary snip. Try to cut only what you need close to the V of a join, and always at a slant if possible.

Here are a few of the materials I love to forage for and where you can expect to find them:

Beech tree branches – Hedgerows

Bracken leaves – Heathland

Hogweed – Road verges

Larch branches – Woodland

Oxeye daisies – Roadside verges and unmanaged strips of land

Rosehips – Hedgerows. Keep an eye out for wild rosebushes throughout the summer and return to them in autumn (fall)

Timothy grasses – Grassland

Wild honeysuckle vines (for wreath bases) – Natural woodlands

Yarrow – Grassland

CREATIVE FORAGING

I've become bold in searching for things, finding opportunities to gather flowers and branches in places I wouldn't have considered previously. Sometimes it takes a little bit of courage when approaching a new foraging situation but I always think 'what's the worst that can happen?'

Have a think about the people you know, the jobs they do and the space they live in. Do you know anyone who's a florist or gardener? Or anyone with a big garden that might be useful when it comes to finding material to dry? Most florists will have waste, and while much of it won't be of use for drying as it may be past its best, there will be instances where they have stock that they would ordinarily throw away and which could be rescued by you. I have a few flower farmer and florist friends who will save me leftovers to collect and dry, which often saves them the job of composting the material.

My garden is relatively small, with limited productivity and volume when it comes to producing dried flowers, so I lean on those that have bigger gardens. In exchange for help pruning a bush or a tree, I can return home with a boot full of eucalyptus branches and other drying materials. Drying flowers needn't be an expensive hobby. Make the most of what nature freely provides us with before investing.

Living in a suburban area may mean you're close to a flower market and can pick up bargain bunches to dry. Delphiniums and huge heads of hydrangea are relatively good value at the height of the season so it's worth having a look and experimenting with a few bunches. Make sure the blooms aren't looking too tired – you want them at their peak to make sure they'll dry well.

THE PROCESS

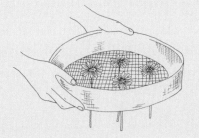

Drying flowers is a joyful experience, and often an experiment! Even now I am thrown by surprises and delights from the results. While there are many methods for drying, and some require more effort than others – my guidance is to start simply to begin whilst you figure things out.

Certain blooms respond better to specific methods and it's worth remembering, when drying materials at home, that results can be inconsistent, so always dry more than you think you will need. Be prepared for some blooms to lose their colour and turn a soft shade of brown. If, like me, you don't mind a bit of vintage charm, see if you can find a use for these less vibrant blooms as filler among the showstoppers.

Don't be afraid to experiment, I've had some of my best successes when breaking the rules.

WHEN TO PICK

Ideally, material should be picked then dried relatively quickly, ensuring that the flowers start the drying process in the best condition. But this doesn't always happen – I pick most of my material and carry the bundles of grasses and seed heads around until I can hang them out. Most things survive this treatment. You should always ensure the material you're planning on drying is free of any moisture. So if you pick in the morning when dew is still on the leaves and petals, give them a chance to dry off properly before you start preparing them. Excess moisture can lead to mould, causing the leaves to turn slimy and preventing the drying process. If I've had to pick when the plants are damp, I'll lay them out to dry on tissue paper or newspaper before hanging them out.

The best stage to dry flowers depends on the look you want, as well as the specific flower. Helicrysum, for example, are as stunning when dried in full bloom as they are when the teeny tiny buds that run down the stems are dried. As a rule, picking flowers in bud won't bring great results – they can succumb to mould because they're too tightly packed to allow air to get in and dry them out. That being said, I have had success when picking for drying later in the season – a rosebud in September or October, for instance – as the plant is already coming to the end of its flowering season.

As a general rule, the best time to pick flowers for drying is when they're at their peak – when the petals have fully opened but aren't yet turning. There are exceptions to this rule; with tall flowers such as delphiniums or loosestrife, I pick the spires when approximately half the flower heads are out with the top parts remaining in bud. You can find more about specific times to pick particular flowers on pages 27–30.

HANGING OUT TO DRY

I find the most effective method is air-drying blooms upside down. I have consistently good results doing this, and it's the simplest way to dry *en masse*, which is a win if you don't have much time.

To prepare flowers for air-drying, begin by stripping all unwanted foliage from the stalks. I tend to leave some of the top foliage surrounding the flower as it adds an extra bit of texture and gives a more natural appearance to arrangements. Gathering a handful of stems together, wind a length of string or twine around them a number of times, securing it with a tight knot at the end, and leaving enough string to form a loop to hang them with. The stems themselves will shrink as they dry, so make sure that you've tied the bunches tightly enough to keep them together, but not so tight that the stems get crushed. Ideally, bunch flowers of the same variety together for ease when you come to use them, or store them in boxes and try to ensure that the flower heads aren't sitting too close together to allow for good air circulation.

UPRIGHT AIR-DRYING

While most plants respond well to drying upside down, there are a few that I always dry with their heads facing upwards. I do this with bigger headed blooms as I find this results in the blooms drying with a more open appearance and, if they have particularly heavy heads, ensures that they don't droop. I use a reclaimed riddle for this. Stripping the stems of all foliage, I slot each stem individually through the small holes until the head of the flower rests on the mesh. I attach a hook in the centre of the riddle or an upside down wooden crate, and hang it in my drying cupboard. If you don't have a riddle then you can use some fine metal mesh or chicken wire secured to a frame – or a cardboard box with holes punched through would do the job, just watch in case any mould sets in.

Flowers that respond really well to this drying method are:

- Sunflowers
- Rudbeckia
- Zinnias
- Oxeye daisies
- Umbellifers (such as fennel or parsley)

Light   Always try to dry your materials in a dark place. It doesn't have to be dark at all times, but the longer the better as light bleaches colour out of flowers. While you'll always see some colour change and softening, it's best to keep this to a minimum to ensure a good lifespan.

Heat   The space you use should be normal room temperature. If your materials are exposed to too much heat they quickly become brittle, making them hard to work with later.

Air   It's really important to dry your flowers in a space that's completely free of moisture in the air. Bundles of blooms or foliage are susceptible to mould and whole bunches can quickly be spoiled if mould sets in.

Most things will have dried within three to five weeks, and can either be left hanging where they are or transferred to storage boxes lined with either newspaper or tissue paper. Avoid placing too many bunches on top of each other, to prevent crushing delicate buds and flower heads, then store them in a dark, dry space until you need them. Materials can last many years stored in this way, although hopefully you'll be to inspired to create with them, rather than leaving them hidden away.

WHERE TO DRY

Drying flowers can take up a lot of space, but if you're only drying the odd bunch there are many ways to do it. Traditionally, people would have used airing cupboards or well ventilated lofts, but these options aren't available for many of us. My favourite spot is the cupboard under the stairs. This used to be a dumping-ground, but I cleared it out and put nails into the backs of the stairs, providing a perfect, staggered hanging set-up – dark, with air circulating through the gaps in our wooden stairs and completely damp-free. Alternatives are the corner of a wardrobe, garage or even a dry, shady shed. If you are really short of space, you can buy flower and herb hangers, which can be hung from hooks in the ceiling. Circular, these hangers have spaces for several bunches to be hung at once. You could also make a display out of your drying material, which is what I do in my studio as I also love to be surrounded by my flowers – a few bunches hung from a foraged piece of silver birch branch can look as stunning as a feature on a wall – just make sure it's not in direct sunlight.

THE LAZY WAY

Possibly the easiest method is dry evaporation. As I mentioned in the introduction, accidentally doing this started my passion for drying flowers. The beauty of it is that you can enjoy the flowers while they dry, and if it doesn't work as you'd hoped, you can just compost them. After stripping the flowers of any unwanted foliage, and definitely anything that sits below the waterline, put the flowers in a vase and add approximately two inches of water. Ensure that the ends of the stalks sit in the water. And then wait – it can take quite a few weeks for the flowers to dry completely. There is no need to top up the water. This method works particularly well

SILICA DRYING

I struggle a little bit with this method but wanted to include it because when it works, it's brilliant. The issue I have is not with the drying but the longevity of the flowers once they are out of the silica: I've found that if the flowers come into contact with moisture they quickly wilt and lose their structure. So be aware that flowers dried in this way may not last as long as those dried in other ways.

Silica gel is a little like a porous sand – it's what's inside those little packets at the bottom of shoe box packaging to make sure that goods are kept free of moisture. The silica works by drawing the moisture out of the petals and leaves while also holding the flower in shape. Because the flowers aren't exposed to any light, air or heat, when this method works, the colour retained can be astounding.

with hydrangeas, which can be fickle when dried in other ways, and gypsophila, spray roses and mimosa respond well too.

ALTERNATIVE METHODS

While air drying is without a doubt the easiest drying method, and my favourite, there are many plants that don't respond well to being dried in this way, so for these I use other techniques.

Silica is available from most good craft stores and online. I recommend fine silica gel, anything larger can cause dents and damage to the delicate petals of blooms such as cosmos and peonies. Most good silica gel comes with coloured beads which change colour as they become full of moisture. Silica gel beads can be reused by drying them out in an oven on a very low heat for a few hours.

Because silica draws moisture in, it must always be kept in an airtight container with a sealable lid. To use this drying method, you'll need to find a container big enough to hold both the flowers and the silica gel with the lid firmly sealed. This method is especially suitable to smaller flowers. It can limit the quantity of flowers that you can dry in one go, but they only take a few days to dry, which makes it an attractive option if you're short of time.

How to dry with silica:

The nature of this method and the intricacies of the flowers used means any blemish or damage to petals will be magnified when the flowers are dried, so only dry the best of the bunch. You can experiment with drying at different stages of blooming – I've had some success drying the buds of field poppies, for example.

- To dry single heads of flowers, spread an inch or two of sand or silica at the base of the container and gently lay the flowers face down. It's important to make sure that all the elements of the flower are completely covered. I use a dry, clean paintbrush to gently cover them, adding a little more silica as you go and continuing until the flower heads and a good proportion of the stem are covered.

- If you want to keep the stems on the flowers to work with later, or you're working with larger heads, then you will need a large amount of silica and a large sealable container; the flower head and stem will need to be laid down and completely covered with silica.

- Because flowers vary in the amount of time they need to dry, it's best to dry the same types of flowers in one container at a time.

- Keep the containers in a dry, preferably warm place while the magic works.

- To remove the flowers from the solution, gently brush away the silica or sand and, if necessary, use tweezers to pull them out. A soft shake can get rid any loose grains, and further brushing with a tiny paintbrush will make sure they're completely free of solution.

- Storage of the finished blooms is really important – moisture will immediately render them floppy and sad-looking, so airtight containers all the way, and ideally keep the flower heads upright rather than on their sides.

Flowers that dry well using this method are:

- Roses
- Cosmos
- Forget-me-nots
- Clematis
- Poppies
- Tulips

You can expect your blooms to dry within three to five days, depending on variety and room temperature.

add structural charm. Pressing flowers takes quite a bit of practice and patience, and the quality of material really matters. Pressing reveals an intricacy and level of detail that would normally go unnoticed and damage to leaves and petals is magnified, so if you go on to frame your blooms, you'll want them to look their absolute best. So it's always best to start with perfect specimens, making sure the petal edges are nibble-free. It's important to press them as soon as you pick them too, otherwise the petals will begin to droop and that will negatively affect the end results.

Most flowers respond well to pressing, with the exception of big, blousy blooms that are too full of moisture or have too many layers to dry out properly, although individual petals can be separated and dried. Daisies,

PRESSING FLOWERS

Most of us have probably done this at some point and felt the joy of discovering a forgotten pressed bloom as it flutters from the pages of a book. While I usually press smaller flowers and leaves, I've recently enjoyed drying bigger branches and ferns. The results can be quite stunning and, when included in arrangements,

nigella, bluebells and poppies will bring you stunning results. Think about the form of the flowers when pressing, you can press the heads alone or the whole stem and leaves for a striking display.

How to use a flower press:

- Prepare your flowers by snipping off any unwanted foliage and make sure they're free of dirt. Use flowers that are in their prime – pressing those that are beginning to turn will result in faded and sometimes wrinkled blooms. If necessary, dry the petals and leaves with kitchen paper or a tea towel to ensure they're totally dry before putting them in the press.

- Lay your flowers, face down, on a fresh piece of blotting paper on the cardboard dividers at the base of your flower press. Carefully push the head of the flower so that it spreads out slightly – you can use weights to hold the flower heads down if they pop up.

- Once all your flower heads are in position, lay a fresh sheet of blotting paper over the top, then layer with the cardboard and screw on the flower press. Tighten the bolts enough to squeeze the flowers flat, but not so much that you damage them.

- Leave the flower press for one to two weeks before unscrewing it and gently lifting the pressed flowers off the blotting paper. The flowers can stick, so be careful – use a pair of tweezers if you need to, to gently prise any delicate petals off the blotting paper to avoid breakages.

- Store in flat large envelopes or cardboard boxes, with the pressed flowers separated with tissue paper.

Alternative methods:

If you don't have a flower press a big book works just as well – as long as you don't mind a few marks on the pages. You can follow the same method as before, using the pages of the book as the blotting paper. Be mindful of how many flowers you place in each book and try to ensure that you leave a good few pages between each pressing to avoid any lumps or bumps showing. Tuck the book away for a few weeks before revealing the pressed flowers.

Pressing the big things

A recent discovery of mine has been pressing large ferns and big branches with the leaves still attached. Best suited to autumn (fall), when the leaves are beginning to turn, whole branches of beech can be pressed, keeping the leaves on the branch and avoiding the curling that normally takes place. I save these leaves and ferns to include in arrangements or wreaths in winter. To keep the leaves and their shapes looking natural and not too flat, you can use quite a bit less pressure than you would for flowers. We have a big rug in our living room and I slot a few layers of leaves and newspaper under there for a few weeks until they're dry. Alternatives are mattresses or any large objects that can apply pressure to the leaves.

Pick your branches and leaves when they're either beginning to turn or are just past their fresh best. Lay them between big sheets of blotting paper or newspaper and place them under a heavy object to allow them to dry.

Plants that respond well to this type of drying are:

- Beech
- Ferns
- Bracken
- Acer

CREATE

THE PROJECTS

The first thing I ever made with dried flowers was a wreath. Back then my style was quite different and I used a technique that was incredibly labour-intensive. Over time I've refined my techniques for making wreaths and discovered how versatile dried flowers can be. I've put together my favourite projects for you to try, with a focus on bringing nature into the home, wearing dried flowers, and using flowers to capture memories of significant events.

While I'd encourage you to develop your own style when creating, there are a few important things to bear in mind:

Working with colour
I find it useful to know what the lead colour will be – everything else can be built up around it. This can be helpful if you're creating something with a specific room in mind so you can be sure it will work in situ.

Dried flowers will lose their vibrancy, so some combinations that wouldn't work for fresh flowers can look stunning with dried. I find I can mix more colours with dried flowers. Think about layering your colours as you would if you were painting in oils – the muted golden tones of autumnal grasses can make your bolder flowers pop.

While you can get dried flowers that have been dyed vibrant colours or bleached white, I avoid them in favour of the natural colours that nature provides. If you want to achieve a bleached look, have a go at drying plants such as ammi and grasses in a bright dry room in the height of the summer – I have had some great successes with this.

Embrace texture

I'm obsessed with texture, from my favourite coffee mug to the crumbling plaster wall in my mum's house, and that of dried flowers. I often find myself gently stroking the heads of my strawflowers or running my fingers through big bunches of quaking grass. I try to bring in as many different textures and flows as possible. Whether rigid blooms alongside flowing grasses or structural poppy heads next to bouncy allium seed-balls, it's the level of detail that interests me. You want people to draw in close to examine what's been used to make the display, and this is achieved through thoughtful consideration of all the elements in the mix.

Fresh-to-dry

You can use fresh flowers in creations that will then dry – the flower crown on page 148 is a good example. You could also give a gift of a bouquet that's part fresh and part dry and which will keep for longer than just a few weeks. And if you work with fresh flowers, as seen in the Garden Gathered Bouquet (page 126) and they don't dry quite as you'd hoped, you can replace them with an alternative.

Keep these guidelines and suggestions in mind as you work through the projects that follow. Allow yourself to work without boundaries and just have a go. Start by grabbing a bunch of flowers from your garden or when you're out for a walk – for me the process is more important than the result. Most of all, enjoy it, savour the time working with dried flowers gives you to be with yourself, calmly, thinking only about what you're doing.

TECHNIQUES

What follows are a few simple techniques and tips that I hope will make creating with dried flowers that little bit simpler. I wasn't taught these techniques and have learnt my way of making things through trial and error, so whilst I hope you will adopt them, if you have a way of doing things which works for you then by all means continue to create that way.

Working with predominantly natural materials means they don't always play ball, and in addition, I find that grasses and long branches, it can become quite a wasteful material to work with. So I have shared with you the way in which I get the most out of my materials, ensuring as little waste as possible, as well as my tried-and-tested ways of working with raffia and wire such as securing and tying off ends.

You will have time on your hands. Time to perfect securing that knot or the stripping and dividing of grass heads. Use this to your advantage and take the time you need to develop and trial the techniques that follow.

MAKING A MINI POSY

As you read through the projects in this book you will notice that many begin with the words 'make a small posy'. This simply means to gather a selection of blooms, seed heads and grasses together to create a small bunch of stems. You don't need to tie these stems together when working with them, it's just a way to start a project and to ensure all the materials work well in their chosen grouping. When gathering your posy, work with roughly 30 per cent main and supporting flower with the remaining 70 per cent made up with foliage, seed heads and grasses.

STRIPPING STEMS

I try to keep my stems as free of leaves as possible; this ensures that the projects you're making don't become too bulky and keeps the base structure easy to work with. It also minimises the risk of mould developing. I prep as I go, working one handed, but if it is easier then it's a good idea to start by stripping your stems before you begin. Simply run your thumb and forefinger down the stalk of your material stripping away unwanted leaves, leaving the top few in place for added interest.

FINISHING A PROJECT WITH STRING OR TWINE

You'll likely want to cover up unsightly stems and wire on some projects, once you have finished. For those instances when a ribbon is too much I use twine or string as an alternative. Starting at the top of the stalks near the flower heads, wrap your twine around the stalks a few times. Lay one length of the twine down against the stalks so it follows their direction. Then working with the opposite length, wind the twine around and around, slowly working your way down until you reach the base of the stalks. You will have met your other end of twine. Now simply tie a double knot to secure.

TYING TWO ENDS OF RAFFIA TOGETHER

For the reasons mentioned before, tying two ends of raffia together requires some skills, or else they easily come loose, as is the nature of the material. You will likely need to do this if using the material to make larger wreaths where one length isn't enough. Take the two ends you wish to connect together and leaving yourself enough length, position them alongside each other with the ends together. Loop both ends of the raffia round your forefinger, back over themselves and then up and through the hole where your forefinger was, pull to tighten the knot.

LOOPING RAFFIA TO SECURE ENDS

I love raffia – although many folks don't! It gets a bad rap but is so useful and is entirely natural. That being said it can be a little hard to work with, it doesn't naturally grip to itself and so securing ends can be bothersome. After many years of frustration I have developed a solid way to secure the end of raffia.

Take the end of the raffia you wish to secure, hold your forefinger over the project end of the raffia, loop the loose end over the top of your finger and wind around, threading the loose end up and through the hole where your forefinger is – pull tightly to secure. This can be completed a number of times if needs be.

SECURING WIRE AND RAFFIA

For many of the makes in this book you will need to secure wire or raffia to the base of your project. I find the easiest way is to wrap the wire around the base a few times and then secure in a knot or twist in the case of wire. A much as possible, I keep the wire and the raffia attached during my makes. I find it much easier and faster than working with individual lengths of wire. But of course, you can work in the way you find the easiest!

SECURING WIRE AT THE END OF A PROJECT

As you reach the end of your project you will need to secure the wire you have been using to stop the project unravelling. Simply take the length of wire you are using, cut it from its reel and gently thread it through the winds of wire you have on your project. Tuck the end in neatly and give the wire a very gentle squeeze to secure it and the end.

DIVIDING LARGE GRASSES AND TALL FLOWERS

For a long while I was put off working with tall grasses such as festuca and taller flowers like delphinium. It seemed a shame to use only part of the flower if all I needed was a small length for one project. So instead, I started to divide the grasses and flowers up. By following the line of the stalk, you will see that many are made up of small off-shoots of grasses and flower heads. One festuca grass head can be split down into 3 or 4 smaller sprigs and the same goes for delphinium or larkspur. You will get much more out of your material by doing this!

WREATHS

I am a firm believer that wreaths aren't just for Christmas, and in many countries they appear on front doors all year round. In the U.S.A it's perfectly normal to have an autumn (fall) wreath on your door, or one made of seashells if you live near the coast. Wreaths can be a display of your personality and style, and they're a beautiful way to welcome guests at your front door, into your home. Here are wreaths that will suit all of your styles and preferences, from traditional to modern. There really is no right or wrong when it comes to wreath-making and I'd encourage you to have a go and enjoy the process as much as the end result.

WREATHS

WORKING WITH THE SEASONS

Traditionally we have used wreaths in the festive season to adorn our front doors and welcome visitors, as well as to mark other seasonal events in the calendar such as Midsummer's Day and May Day.

I'm a firm believer in wreaths having a place in our homes and on our doors no matter the season. It seems such a waste when Christmas or Thanksgiving wreaths are taken down so soon after the festivities. That's why I always make my Christmas wreaths to last. When I run workshops, I provide my guests with fresh foliage and berries but always with longevity in mind, so that the wreaths people have taken such care in creating will last beyond December.

I'm frequently asked about the types of material that can be used in wreath making, so on page 65 I've given a few of my favourite forage materials for autumn (fall) and winter wreath-making as well as my favourite base materials.

Essentially all you need to make the base of a wreath is a good quantity of a vine that's flexible enough to bend into a circle (of sorts) and that will ideally strengthen as it dries. There are so many options out there, each providing a different look and feel.

Autumn to me is all about the golden hues of the leaves as they begin to turn and the growth of the natural world slows down, when the sun dips lower in the sky and she lights up the leaves on the trees and the remaining flower heads in one last burst of glory before winter. This is my favourite season. While many see it as a shift towards darker months, I see it as a season of new beginnings. Nature does a grand job of drying things for me, so the options available for creating are endless, unlike in summer, when things are generally too fresh to work with.

You can easily create a wreath in autumn using branches plucked fresh from a tree and leave it hanging on your wall to watch the leaves turn naturally.

BASE MATERIALS

- *Hops* – These are my absolute favourite to make wreath-bases with. The ideal time to pick them is mid-autumn (fall) when the tendrils are still bendy but not so soft that they snap. They're a bit of a beast to grow because of how vigorous they can be, so I get mine from our local brewery who are happy to give up the vines instead of having to incinerate them. The beauty of the hop vine is that it dries so hard and tough you can use it to make the biggest of wreaths without worrying that it will collapse.

- *Wild honeysuckle* – You can find this growing in woodlands across the U.K. This vine is easily spotted as it snakes its way up a tree trunk towards the light. With a bit of yanking you can cut the base of a vine and rip the length down to take away. Honeysuckle makes wonderful wild and wayward wreath-bases, and is less uniform in its structure than hops.

- *Birch branches* – Look out for the long droopy branches which are more likely to be found in woodland than on birch trees standing alone. A beautiful birch branch can be transformed into a free spirit of a wreath-base where the loose ends make up part of the end design. The best time to pick them is autumn, when the leaves are just beginning to turn.

- *Virginia creeper* – I adore the cute little swirls this plant throws out to grip onto its base. As the vine is that much smaller on virginia creeper, I tend to use it for mini-wreaths (page 78) and smaller traditional wreaths. It will need some drying time before using it.

- *Clematis* – Similar in many ways to wild honeysuckle, the vines of clematis, particularly slightly older ones, have an intriguing aged texture with strips of bark falling off – it makes for a wonderful, on-point autumnal wreath-base.

- *Willow* – Not a favourite of mine, only because it tends (when you can manipulate it correctly) to make picture-perfect circular wreaths and that just isn't my style. Still, it's a solid, long-lasting choice for a wreath-base.

AUTUMNAL WREATH INSPIRATION

- Beech branches with the leaves still on
- Hydrangea heads as their petals begin to brown
- Bracken in all its crispy glory (flatten slightly before use)
- Birch branches
- Fluffy clematis seed heads
- Rose hips
- Teasel heads
- Chinese lanterns
- Honesty

WINTER WREATH INSPIRATION

- Larch branches
- Lichen-covered twigs
- Pine cones and fir cones
- Ilex leaves and berries
- Sacred bamboo – leaves and berries
- Pistache – available from flower markets and florists
- Newly forming catkin buds
- Eucalyptus
- Juniper

EVERLASTING

FLORAL WREATH

GATHER

- Raffia

- A vine wreath-base measuring roughly 25 cm (10 in) – I make my own but you can buy them online from places such as Hobbycraft. Here, I used a virginia creeper vine

- A selection of 3–5 types of foliage and seed heads – I used festuca grasses, asparagus fern andphalaris grass heads

- One type of lead flower – I used ammobium

- 1–2 types of supporting flowers – I used rhodanthe

- Twine, silk ribbons

This is the wreath that started Botanical Tales and will always hold a special place in my heart. My style has evolved over the years, as has the method I use to create them.

The early wreaths were delicate and dainty and made laboriously by threading the stems of flowers through the wreath-base. My wreaths have become bigger and bolder over the years, and while they're still a labour of love, the technique I use now is much easier to master.

These wreaths are entirely natural and can be thrown on the compost once their days are done. Having said that, they will last many years in a suitable place.

LET'S GET STARTED

1. Begin by taking your length of raffia and tying it securely to a suitable place on your wreath-base.

2. Prepare your materials by stripping away any unwanted leaves from the stems and trimming the lengths if necessary (see techniques, page 57). I tend to keep a bit of length in the stalk – I find it helps to ensure that everything is held securely in place.

3. When building the wreath, try to leave the foliage and seed heads with enough of their stalks free to have some movement – if you pull them too tightly together the wreath may end up with too much bulk at the front and not enough movement. The same can happen if the raffia is positioned too close to the top of the seed heads or the flowers. If you leave enough of the stalk present above where it is held in place, it will allow you to tweak their position later in the wreath-making.

4. Working with mini-posies, gather a few stems of your foliage and seed heads together, positioning them in such a way that all the elements have room to breathe and show through – forming a sort of fan-shape with the material works well (see techniques, page 57).

5. Lay a posy over the top of where you've secured the raffia to the base and then, using the loose end of raffia, secure the posy to the wreath-base a few times by wrapping the raffia around it.

   Continue building up your wreath with your mini-posies, bringing in your main and supporting flowers at a rate of roughly one third to two thirds of foliage. You want to be working round the wreath in slight increments as you go, paying attention to how the material lies on the wreath base to ensure all sides of the wreath are building up at a similar rate.

6. Secure each posy by wrapping the raffia around it a few times. If your raffia gets too short to work with, tie another piece in place (see techniques, page 58).

7. How far you go around the wreath is up to you – I normally know when mine are finished by holding them up against a wall to see how they look when hanging.

8. When you're happy with the shape of your wreath, you will need to secure both the final stalks and the raffia. Wrap your raffia around the base of your stalks a few times and secure the end using the technique on page 58.

9. Take a look at the ends of your material – sometimes I leave them long and trim them down to make them a little tidier – this can create a good balance in the wreath. Otherwise you will need to trim them all the way down to just below the bottom of the raffia.

10. Play around with raffia, ribbons and twine to finish the wreath off. You can use the material to cover up the raffia and stalks and bring a different texture to the design, or you can use a ribbon with long ends hanging down. Alternatively, you can tie another length of raffia round for simple, natural beauty.

CONTEMPORARY

WREATH ON A BRASS HOOP

GATHER

- Florist wire

- A metal hoop – I source mine from independent suppliers such as workshop.ltd or Rowen & Wren

- Selection of grasses, foliage and seed heads; here I used eucalyptus nicoli and asparagus fern as the base with amaranthus, everlastings and alchemilla mollis

- Selection of flowers – the lighter the better for this wreath

- Length of naturally dyed ribbon or soft cloth

You can use any metal base or wooden hoop to recreate this modern take on a traditional wreath.

My home is minimalistic-comfort in style, inspired by our time in the Netherlands, so a brass base looks stunning as a stand-alone piece on a bare wall.

The bases can be re-used many times, so can reflect the changing of the seasons.

LET'S GET STARTED

1. Taking your florist wire, attach one end to the metal hoop securely by wrapping it round tightly and then twisting it back on itself. The wire may shift along the base ever so slightly, but this should stop happening when you begin adding in material (see techniques, page 59).

2. Choose a selection of filler materials such as foliage and seed heads and gather them in a mini-bunch. To avoid the different flowers sitting on top of each other, fan the stems apart before you place them on top of the secured wire on the hoop. Keeping the wire attached, wrap it round the stems a few times to keep them in place. Try not to pull the stems too much when wrapping the wire as you want them to remain open as much as possible.

   I tend to work roughly in thirds, two thirds with the foliage and filler, such as the seed heads and grasses, and a third main flower and supporting flowers. I try as much as possible to be free with the placement of my flowers rather than formulaic, but follow your intuition.

3. Continuing to build the wreath by overlaying mini-bunches of blooms as you go, pay attention to the sides as well as the front-facing part of the wreath. Work with the flow of the stems and use bushier elements to cover up any wire that may be showing.

   How far you go around the base is up to you, but one thing to bear in mind is that when creating an asymmetrical wreath on a metal base such as this, *the wreath will naturally fall to where the weight is*. The lighter the material you use, the less this will happen, but it's worth remembering as you will need to be flexible with the way it hangs to avoid disappointment.

4. When you're happy with the structure of your wreath, you'll need to finish off the ends, working with the same length of wire as you have been the whole way round, wrapping it around the ends of your material a few times before securing it tightly at the back of the wreath. Cut the wire free and tuck any loose ends into the wire wraps (see techniques, page 58).

5. Finish the wreath with a length of ribbon or cloth, using it to cover the wire and suit the wreath to the room it will be hung in.

   Wire wreaths can be hung on front doors, but consider how they might bang against the door when you shut it – this can damage wooden doors over time, so be careful.

WILD & WAYWARD

WREATH

GATHER

- 2 large, flexible branches of birch or beech

- Florist wire

- A selection of tall, flowing or fluffy grass seed heads such as Phragmites australis

- A handful of turning bracken, not too crisp, with a bit of flexibility left in it

- 4 honesty stems

- Naturally dyed ribbon – a number of different lengths and shades

I adore autumn (fall) and everything that comes with it – the changing colour of the leaves, the softening of the light as the long days of summer slowly slip away and the gradual shift in the pace of daily life.

From the middle of August I come home with my arms or my car full of foraged finds to hang out to dry. Wild and wayward wreaths can be created instantly with finds at this time of year, most of which will be on their way to naturally drying out. This method of wreath-making is so simple and can be achieved in a very short time, with stunning results.

LET'S GET STARTED

1. The two branches are used to form your wreath-base. Start by taking the thick ends and connect them by wrapping a length of florist wire around the stems tightly (see techniques, page 59). Looping the branch ends into a circle, secure them together at the bushy ends with another length of wire – loosely enough for the circle to have movement and for the branch ends to be relatively free – you want to leave some ends to flow out to the sides.

2. Working with individual lengths of wire, start to secure your seed heads and bracken branches, layering up over the thick ends of the branches, securing them to the main base of the wreath. With this style of wreath, I have worked from a central point, out in opposite directions, creating a fan that looks effective with the foliage.

3. Once you have the base of the foliage in place, add in your flower and grass heads over the top to bring a lightness to the wreath, keeping them evenly spaced to allow the seed heads to shine through.

4. Finally, using the ribbons, tie big bows with lengths of ends hanging down from the central point – I've used two different lengths of ribbon on mine for a flowing finish.

EXTRA

INSPIRATION

Have fun! There is no structure to these kinds of wreaths and therefore the most fun to make.

Have a play around with different fabrics to make more of the central focal point.

Create a festive wreath in this style by using plenty of evergreen, holly berries and other nature finds. Finish with a brass cow bell.

Ivy vines and clematis would work beautifully in this kind of wreath.

MINI DRIED

FLOWER WREATHS

GATHER

- Thin, flexible vines such as virginia creeper or clematis

- A length of raffia

- A selection of loose grasses, seed heads and flowers

- Ribbon, twine or fabric, to decorate (optional)

I started making mini wreaths to use up odds and ends I had from larger sized ones, but the mini versions soon became the most popular wreaths I make.

I now make them as wall hangings – they look beautiful hung as a collection, as well as for place settings at weddings, and to decorate wrapped gifts.

LET'S GET STARTED

1. Take your vines, which need to be flexible enough to wind round into a 5–10 cm (2–4 in) circle. Form the size of circle you want with one end of the vine. Hold it closed between your thumb and forefinger while you wind the other end through and round to build up a solid but delicate wreath-base. I wind it so that there are at least three lengths of vine in any one place. Take the loose end of the vine and tuck it in and through the existing structure to hold it in place.

2. Taking your length of raffia, tie it in a double knot around the section of wreath where the loose end is tucked in. This ensures that the wreath base doesn't ping open, which can happen with this kind of vine base (see techniques, page 59).

3. Working with your selection of dried materials, gather a small bunch and lay it over the top of the raffia knot. Holding it in position with your thumb and forefinger, wrap the loose end of raffia around the base of the flowers a couple of times and gently pull it tight. Take care to not wrap the raffia too high up on the stems – you want the flowers to have enough freedom to be tweaked into position and to have a bit of flower about them (see techniques, page 59).

4. For my mini wreaths, I tend to only fill about a third of the wreath-base, and often end up with a design that resembles a mini bouquet. I find that less is more with these wreaths, allowing me to appreciate the beauty of the tiny flowers I use.

5. Once you're happy with your design, carefully wrap the raffia around the base of the last bunch of flowers to secure the stems, tie in a knot at the back by looping the loose end through one of the wrapped sections, and pull tight (see techniques, page 58).

The raffia can form part of the design or, alternatively you could take a length of twine, ribbon or thin strip of fabric to finish off the piece.

EXTRA

INSPIRATION

Use these wreaths to decorate place settings at a dinner party or a gift for a loved one.

Create a collection of mini wreaths on a bedroom wall for a nature-inspired wreath montage.

Use as favours at your wedding, by allowing your guests to take one home at the end of the night.

IN THE HOME

Dried materials can bring depth and interest to your home, softening stark rooms with their textures and tones and at the same time keeping you connected to nature. This feels particularly important in the dark months of winter, when the time we spend outside is more limited. Dried flowers are then a reminder of what will come when longer days return and nature reasserts herself. Dried flower displays can help to keep hopeful, joyful feelings alive through the dark winter.

SEASONAL

BOTANICAL MOBILE

GATHER

- Flower heads or seed heads of your choice – here I've used chinese lanterns

- Organic cotton, hemp or thin strips of naturally dyed material

- A large branch with leaves still attached, or lots of tendrils in place, such as birch or beech

This is a perfect make for when autumn (fall) arrives in all its golden glory and the leaves are just beginning to turn.

When I shared an image of this on Instagram, one of my followers commented that they thought it looked like hearts were falling from the branch, and it made me love it even more! This mobile looks extra-special when made using materials that catch the light throughout the day.

Any branch will do, but a favourite of mine is to use a beech branch with leaves still attached so that they curl and brown naturally.

LET'S GET STARTED

1. Prepare your seed or flower heads by stripping them of any unwanted leaves or foliage (see techniques, page 57). This mobile benefits from simplicity and the negative space created, so less is definitely more. Make sure you leave enough stem to tie the thread to, but no more.

2. Tie a piece of thread to the end of each flower head, making sure they are all secure. Don't worry too much about the length, as this will be determined by the position of each one on the branch.

3. Take the ribbon and tie each end to a suitable place on the branch that will give you a loop to hang it with. I find it easiest to hang the branch from a hook as I position the flower heads – this way you can better see any gaps that need to be filled.

4. When your branch is hanging, tie on your flower or seed heads. You want to aim for a good balance of lengths and distances between each hanging, and give everything space to breathe and be taken in – don't overdo it. This creation benefits from its simplicity, so try your best not to clutter it.

5. Hang it from a corner or wall that gets natural light to let it have good visual impact.

MEADOWSCAPE

TABLE DECORATIONS

GATHER

- A small branch roughly 4–6 cm (2–3 in) in diameter, cut into lengths ranging from 10–15 cm (5–7 in). I love silver birch for this, as well as logs that have lichen on the bark

- A drill with a 1–2 mm (#60–#47) drill bit

- Structural grasses and seed heads – I used quaker grasses, fox tail grasses, bunnies tail grasses, as well as burnet wildflowers and cow parsley seed heads

Decorating dinner tables with dried flowers is a cost-effective and time-efficient way of bringing personality and style to a dinner party or event.

The beauty of dried flowers is that they can be arranged on the morning of the event or weeks beforehand – perfect if you will be in a hurry and have guests walking through the door the moment you get home from work. With no danger of wilting, you can be really inventive in how you use them.

The method here is one that I first used when I was putting together a large-scale meadowscape at Strawberry Hill House in Twickenham, London. I wanted to create the feel of walking through a meadow in midsummer. For that installation I used large planks of reclaimed wood and much bigger chunks of wood than I have here, but the method was the same.

LET'S GET STARTED

1. Once you have enough lengths of branch cut to provide cover for your table, drill small holes in each log on one of the cut sides with the fine drill. The depth of the hole should be roughly 5 cm (2½ in) to allow for enough stalk to sit inside it and balance the seed or flower head.

2. Drill between 5 and 10 holes in each cut section of branch.

3. Laying the logs out, in position, on your table, start by filling the holes with your dried material. I like to work with the sections of wood in situ, so I can see how

the whole thing builds up as I go. Work with one material at a time, to give your table an even, gathered appearance. Use a range of different lengths of stalk for interest and flow. Keep going, adjusting and adding until you are happy with the depth and height of your display.

4. The beauty of a display like this is that it is open enough for guests to be able to see each other across the table while they're dining, so height isn't an issue. Add candles, ensuring none are creating a fire hazard.

INSPIRATIONAL

PLACE SETTINGS

These place-setting decorations can really lift the appearance of a table, whether for a dinner party at home or a wedding celebration.

When I hosted supper clubs, each of my guests took away either a mini-wreath or dried flower posy – a beautiful keepsake from a wonderful time with friends.

Create the mini dried-flower posies, following the same principles as those on page 146 for boutonnières, and for the tutorial for mini dried flower wreaths on page 78. You can limit yourself to one design or make them all a little different – whichever you'd prefer.

ETHEREAL

FLOWER GARLANDS

GATHER

- Bullion wire

- A selection of seed, flower and grass heads

- A structure to hang them from –
  I used a riddle for mine

This make is one of the simplest yet most effective to create. It's a great way to use up all those loose flower heads that you'll have after creating.

There is no need to buy flowers specifically for this creation. Flower garlands can be used to add interest and texture to wall displays when hung individually among pictures and paintings, and also look stunning hung, en mass, as a display. I decorated my local Oxfam bookshop's window with a display using this method, so people walking past could see through the flowers into the treasure-trove of the shop beyond.

1. Cut a length of your wire – roughly 30 cm (12 in) or dependent on the space you are wishing to fill.

2. Starting at one end, begin to wrap the wire around the stalk of a flower a few times. As stalks can be brittle, try to be as gentle as possible to avoid snapping them.

3. Work with the flowers as close or as far apart as you wish, trying to leave space for each bud to show.

4. Continue until you have a number of lengths of wire-wrapped blooms.

5. Hang in your chosen spot, either direct from the ceiling or from a structure such as a riddle or even a foraged branch.

EXTRA

INSPIRATION

Keep hold of all your spare flower heads and broken stems in cool, dry place to create with later.

Branches of bracken and fern can be divided up and look beautiful in the light.

Seed heads such as honesty and nigella work really well.

If you are short on space, you could create a similar display by using a thin strip of fabric with mini bunches of flowers with cotton twine.

EVERLASTING

FLORAL DISPLAY

GATHER

- Chicken wire

- An old vessel such as an urn or open-necked vase

- Florist tape

- A selection of dried material – consider not just the colour combination but the textures and flow of the display; here I used hawthorn branches, festuca grasses, bracken, teasel seed heads, twisted rudbeckia flower heads, Queen Anne lace flowers and seeds with a sprinkling of micanthus

Dried flowers make interesting, unique and long-lasting displays for the house.

Aside from the many projects you will find in this book, you can also display dried flowers in the same way as fresh ones.

Pampas grass has become popular recently, and a few stalks of it placed in a large enamel jug is a simple, effective way to lift a dark corner. Similarly, structural seed heads such as amni are understated, but breathtaking nevertheless when displayed in a tiny vessel. Arrange a number of these on a mantlepiece or window ledge.

For displays in vessels such as urns or open-necked vases, I find it easiest to work with a base of chicken wire to keep the stems in position. With no water to hold them, it's tricky to achieve an attractive display without structural support.

LET'S GET STARTED

1. Form a dome out of chicken wire, snug enough to sit securely in the vessel and make sure roughly a third of the dome sits above the opening of the vessel. Place a cross of tape over the top of the vessel to hold the chickenwire in place.

2. Before you begin, consider where your vessel is going to be – for example, will all of the sides be visible, or will it be front-facing on a mantlepiece?

3. Begin with bulkier materials first, putting them in place to form the main structure – aim for an L-shape or sideways-lying tick to give an interesting balance to the display.

4. Once your main flowers are in place, introduce the filler flowers or seed heads. Use different lengths of stems to conceal the chicken wire. Follow the natural flow of the stems and leaves, introducing floppy, soft grass-heads to soften any hard structural elements of the display.

5. Now add the smallest, most delicate of your of dried materials, gypsophila for example. Dot the stems of these flowers about your main structure to bring the display together as one complete vision.

6. Put the display in the place you're going to keep it and make any final additions and adjustments, adding more stems if required and repositioning the jar.

EXTRA

INSPIRATION

When using a vessel as large as this one, you can place an upturned flower pot at the base before adding the chicken wire.

Try using both fresh and dried material for this display – here I used hawthorn berries, which will dry over time, becoming a little wrinkly and more muted in colour.

Break up the solid branches and seed heads with flowing grasses and twisted flower heads.

Switch up your materials if they get tired by carefully lifting out spent stems and replacing with fresh ones.

AUTUMNAL

WALL HANGING

GATHER

- A big, beautiful branch – the more imperfect the better as it gives the material you hang from it a supporting grip – or, alternatively, a few branches with leaves or seed heads on them, such as beech or birch, which can be wired together to make the base. Mine is copper beech

- Florist wire

- A selection of pressed or fresh leaves, seed heads and flowers of your choice, all should be at least the length of your branch. I used asparagus fern, autumnal-toned everlastings, dried feverfew and some strands of amaranth

- A length of naturally dyed cloth

Hanging boughs are really simple to make and are a wonderful alternative to wreaths.

You can make them as free-flowing as you like, or go for a more structured look, but the method remains the same. Boughs can also be made using fresh material and allowed to dry in situ, as I have done here.

LET'S GET STARTED

1. Start by positioning your main branch, or the few branches you have gathered into a solid base. Consider which side to make the top, and whether you need to trim any side-shoots. If you're using a few branches, tie them together securely with your florist wire (see techniques, pages 58–59).

2. Start to layer up your bough, adding more of your selected materials in as uniform or haphazard a way as you like.

3. Once you're happy with the main structure of your bough, wrap the wire round a number of times. This wire will be where you feed in the stems of the other materials, so make sure you have enough loops of wire to accommodate them all. Secure the ends of the wire (see techniques, page 59).

4. Now add in your remaining flowers and seed heads, slotting them along the base of the bough and between the wire loops. Fill any gaps, paying attention to the weight of the bough – if it's too heavy on one side, the bough will pull down that way when hanging. This isn't necessarily a problem, but it will have an impact on the final display.

5. Finally, tie each end of your length of naturally dyed cloth around the bough so you have a loop, and hang it in position.

6. You can also use these as mantlepiece decorations or centrepieces above tables.

DRIED FLOWER

HANGING BOUQUET

GATHER

- A main focal bloom or seed head – I've used allium and hydrangea

- A base of foliage and a selection of twisty, twirly grasses, seed heads and twigs to complement – I've used eucalyptus leaves, statice, achillea and atriplex

- Florist wire

- A length of ribbon or soft, flowing cloth

Displaying bouquets of flowers on the wall like this can be a great way to dry flowers in place as well as displaying bigger blooms such as cardoons or globe artichokes.

Interesting leaves such as palms and holm oaks look beautiful in these displays – their leaves crinkling and curling around the main focal-point as they dry makes for a special multi-dimensional display.

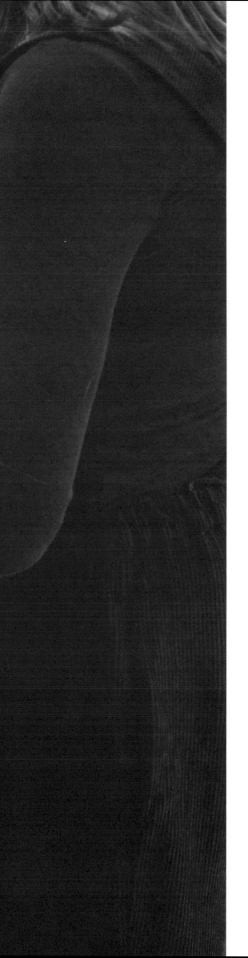

LET'S GET STARTED

1. Starting with your main, focal flower, as you would with a fresh flower arrangement, hold it upright and begin to layer-up foliage and other materials above and around it. Remember that the bunch will be hung from a wall, and therefore needs to be entirely front-facing and as flat as possible at the back.

2. I like to make mine as multi-dimensional as possible, with lots of depth from the centre down and to the sides. Think about using more delicate, twiggy material to shoot out from the sides and the top to avoid the bouquet looking too bulky. As you work, flip the bouquet upside down once in a while, to check how it will look when it's in place. You'll want to use material that holds its shape well. The trouble with using only grasses, for example, is that you will end up with a long, droopy bouquet with less weight around the middle.

3. Once you're happy with the bouquet, secure it with a length of florist wire as tightly as you can without compromising the structure – the stems need to be securely in place so they don't fall out, but equally not tied so tightly that they no longer follow your design.

4. Wrap your ribbon around the wire a couple of times to cover it up, then leave the ends hanging down loosely. Hang in place with a nail and tweak as necessary.

WITH LOVE

It's easy to capture memories and moments in this digital age when most of us have high-quality cameras in our mobile phones. Thousands of photos are stored in them, most of which we'll never look at.

Creating displays of flowers for a special day, which are then dried and pressed, is a grounding experience, one that promises to evoke memories and emotions long after the day has passed.

I've made pressed flower frames from flowers picked on the day of the birth of my goddaughter. A dome jar filled with dried flowers from the garden of our first family home sat on my bedside table for years as a reminder of how far we have come.

Take the time, on these special days, to pause, reflect and pick a few blooms for drying and creating with. You and your loved ones will appreciate them much more than any bought gift.

PRESSED FLOWER

FRAMES

GATHER

- A selection of pressed flowers, such as pansies, nigella, cornflower and cosmos

- Natural glue

- Tweezers

- Wooden skewer

- A wooden or metal picture frame

Pressing flowers is a favourite hobby of mine, but for a long while the flowers I had pressed stayed hidden between the pages of heavy old books and in my flower press.

I wanted to find a way to display them, to remind me of the visit to Wales where I pressed delicate harebells from the mountainside, and the trip to Menorca with days spent on the beach with my family.

I stumbled across these frames on Pinterest – they have no back and can display the pressed flowers in all their beauty. It's possible to make your own frames, or to use delicate metal frames from India, which are easily available worldwide now.

LET'S GET STARTED

1. I always start by laying my pressed flowers out in front of me and carefully selecting the best of them, having a play-around with the structure of the picture I want to create. I do this on a white piece of paper so I can visualise how the frame will look when hung on a wall.

   I'm a big fan of negative space in these designs, so I tend to leave gaps between each flower, but you needn't follow my direction on this.

2. Once you're happy with your layout, tip a small amount of the natural glue onto a small dish and, starting from one end of the design, pick each flower up individually with the tweezers, placing small dots of the glue onto one or two parts of the flower by using the wooden skewer dipped in glue.

   Because the frame has no back, any glue that seeps out when it's placed down will be visible through the glass. For that reason it's really important that you use just the teeniest amount, enough to hold the flower in place and no more.

3. Once all the flowers are in place, leave them for a good hour to let the glue set before placing the top frame of glass in place. Clip the frame together and hang on a wall or from a light-fitting where the natural light will catch the beauty of the flowers.

DOME JAR

WITH DRIED FLOWERS

GATHER

- A selection of dried flowers, seed heads and grasses including loose flower heads - I selected all the flowers that I was most proud of growing: celosia flamingo feather, pink rhodanthe, poppy buds and seed heads, glitter thistles and gomphrena

- A glass dome jar with a wooden base

- Horticultural scissors

- A vintage frog pin

I adore making these dome jars – they can capture a moment in time perfectly, like a wild flower meadow in summer, or here where I have used a selection of the home grown blooms I am most proud of growing this season! A positive reminder of the growing year.

I use a frog pin to make mine, as they can be reused, and if you can find a vintage pin it will look beautiful in itself. If it's a gift, you might want to secure the frog pin to the base of the dome with a dot of superglue.

When selecting the materials, consider what you want to evoke – perhaps your garden in midsummer, or the beauty of the leaves turning in autumn (fall). I find this helps me with the structure and flow, almost as if I'm painting with flowers.

LET'S GET STARTED

1. Begin by measuring the stems against the height of the dome jar and cut each one down so that it's at least 1 cm (½ in) shorter than the distance between the base of the dome jar and its uppermost point.

   Work from the middle outwards, placing the tallest and most prominent flower right in the middle of the frog pin.

   Working with the other materials, build up and around your central bloom. Depending on where you're going to display your dome jar, it can be a front-facing design with all the tall flowers at the back, or one that can be viewed from any angle.

2. Go with the flow of the flowers, a higgledy-piggledy approach is a perfect representation of nature and gives the impression of a garden inside a dome. Give each flower room to breathe and be taken in, and make sure that you bring some interest to draw the eyes to the bottom of the display.

   Cut tips of long flowers off to use as filler, dot dried leaves among the flowers as a soft gap-filler, and consider scattering seeds or petals across the wooden bottom for added interest.

3. Gently place the glass dome over the top of the flowers, taking care to not catch any stems as you do so. The flowers can remain under the glass for years and years free from dust and any risk of damp damage.

EXTRA

INSPIRATION

I've also used natural clay as a base for this – choose one that air-dries quickly to avoid the stems of the flowers rotting.

If you are creating this for yourself at home, don't use superglue to attach the frog pin, because then you will be able to reuse both the pin and dome base again in separate makes.

For a dramatic take, cram the jar full of statuesque flowers such as teasel heads, palm leaves and other graphic dried flowers.

At Christmas time, create a festive display using evergreens and berries, adding in fairy lights for extra sparkle.

DISPLAY

V E S S E L S

- A selection of small blooms and other interesting plant material

- A selection of clean, clear glass vessels such as old medicine jars and chemistry flasks

- A pair of tweezers

- Tall cocktail sticks or metal skewers

- Cork board to cut a lid for the vessel

- Twine or naturally dyed ribbon (optional)

Collections of dried flower vessels look lovely on a shelf.

This is a great way to use up some of the less than perfect blooms or short-stemmed grasses that you may have lying around. They're super-simple to make but visually stunning. These vessels are also a beautiful make to create with children or friends; just gather a few nature finds on a walk and fill a vessel or a simple jam jar!

Many of my vintage glass jars and vessels are lucky finds from antiques markets and charity shops. Keep your eyes peeled when you're at car-boot or yard sales – it's often when you're not looking that they come your way. Etsy and Facebook Marketplace can also be good places to find them.

LET'S GET STARTED

1. Once your flowers are in the vessels, it's tricky to get them out again, so a little bit of pre-planning and visualising is required. With these designs you also need to work from the bottom up.

2. Start by carefully poking the blooms you want to sit on the base of the vessel through the hole at the top. Push flowers through from the base upwards so the petals naturally fold in – this will help to avoid breakages of petals.

3. Build up the display by adding longer stems of blooms and grasses. I find that the more soft, flowy flowers and grasses work best for these displays. Use tweezers and a skewer to gently tease stems into place, using the sides of the vessel to balance the stalks in position.

4. Continue until you're happy with the display, then replace the lid of the vessel, if it has one, or cut a piece of cork to fit the hole. If you like, you can decorate the vessel further by tying a strip of twine or very thin ribbon around the top.

GARDEN

GATHERED BOUQUET

GATHER

- A selection of dried flowers in complementary colours, with one type of statement flower larger than the other supporting blooms. I used ninebark branches, celosia, love lies bleeding, field grasses, dried marjoram and allium seed heads. Fresh mint sprigs and flower heads also featured for a more fragrant bouquet

- A length of raffia

- Naturally dyed silk ribbons (optional)

Giving a gift of a bunch of dried flowers gathered from your garden or foraged from a field is a more thoughtful and sustainable option than buying fresh.

There's no danger of it wilting or deteriorating before it's put in water, and it will give the person who receives it months of joy.

You can go as bold or as dainty as you like when creating these bouquets – my autumn (fall) bunches tend to be much larger than those that I can put together in the depths of winter.

LET'S GET STARTED

1. When gathering your materials, consider the form of the flowers as well as their colours. You will want a mixture of sturdy stems and those that have a flow to them such as soft grasses. Consider wide-open seed heads, such as those from ammi, which can be used to give scale to the bouquet.

2. As dried flowers tend to be more rigid than fresh, I tend to start with a sturdy branch of foliage such as fresh mint or ninebark to form the base structure of my bouquet.

3. Working with your other selected materials, gradually build the bouquet up, ensuring that you work in the same direction with the stems so that they will support each other and stay in place.

4. Build up flowers around the main structure, keeping an eye out for any gaps to be filled. Seed heads and grasses with sturdy stems can easily be slotted into the top of the bouquet to fill gaps without fear of breaking their stems. The aim is to work downwards with each bloom or filler that you add, to finish with a bouquet that's full from all angles.

5. To secure the bunch, take a length of raffia and wind it round the base of the stems in the middle where your hand has been holding them in place. Tighten the raffia then tie it in a double knot.

6. Leave as is for a natural look, or tie the bouquet with a beautiful botanically dyed silk ribbon for that something extra.

THANK YOU

CARDS

GATHER

- Small, pressed flower heads
  with stalks and leaves attached
  (see pages 48–49); I normally work with
  violas, larkspur and nigella flowers

- Washi tape

- Blank, recycled folded cards

*Thank you cards are a ritual
I swear by, despite how easy it
is to send a quick email or text.*

My dad encouraged us to do this after
birthdays and Christmases and the habit
has stayed with me.

Picking and pressing flowers really fixes
a moment, so doing it on a special day,
then sharing the pressed flowers with the
people who came to your celebration seems
fitting to me.

LET'S GET STARTED

1. Start by selecting your favourite and
   most perfect of blooms. Trim them if
   necessary to ensure the fit on the space
   of the card.

2. Lay the flowers in position then tear
   thin strips of washi tape – I tend to tear
   mine widthways as well as lengthways
   to give a more delicate look –then
   carefully lay two strips over the flower
   to secure it in place. I use a thin black
   pen and write the date and flower type
   in the corner of the folded card before
   writing my message.

WEARABLES

Floral wearables have become more popular in recent years, and brides often choose floral hair combs and bracelets over jewellery. The benefit of choosing dried flowers over fresh is that they don't wilt, and look as fresh at the end of the night as they did when the party started.

Floral crowns are great for weddings and other big, festive events, and floral hair combs are perfect for smaller events. Select colours and tones that reflect your personality and style to express yourself in your look. And be bold and proud of the florals you wear.

EVERLASTING

FLORAL BROOCH

GATHER

- A selection of very small flowers on their stalks, in complementary colours and tones – here I've used scabious stellata seed head as the focal point, sea lavender and feverfew as supporting flowers, with a single head of white acrolinium

- Florist wire

- A vintage or brass kilt pin or brooch (I get mine from Etsy)

- A small length of naturally dyed silk ribbon

These brooches are perfect for every day. An easy way to style up a blouse or jacket with your favourite blooms.

You'll need to work with flowers and foliage that's relatively sturdy. Brooches can get knocked, which may cause damage if blooms with very delicate stalks are used. I usually include a seed head of some kind to form a more solid base for the mini bunch.

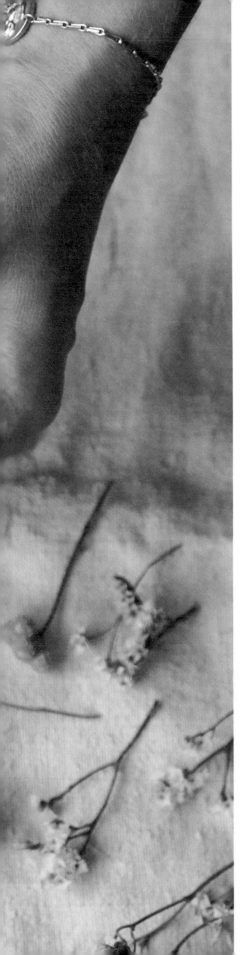

1. Begin by choosing the main focal point –
   this is likely to be your lead flower or
   seed head. It will be the flower that
   has the most prominence when it's in
   position. Build up small sprigs of other
   materials around the feature flower
   head until you have what looks like
   a miniature bouquet. Check that the
   arrangement has flow around the edges
   and to the top, as once it's placed on your
   clothing, you'll want the display to fan
   out and lie neatly on the fabric.

2. Take a length of florist wire, then gently
   wrap it round the stalks of the bouquet
   until you feel they're held together
   securely. Lay the bouquet on top of the
   pin-free section of the brooch and wrap
   another length of florist wire around
   it until the brooch and flowers are held
   together as one.

3. In order to cover the florist wire, which
   will be visible at the base of the brooch,
   select a small, thin length of naturally
   dyed silk ribbon and wrap round a few
   times before tying it in a very small
   knot at the top. Leave the ends loose and
   slightly crumpled for a more casual piece.

DRIED FLOWER

HAIR COMB

GATHER

- A selection of delicate dried flowers, seed heads, and foliage on its stems, such as ruscus, poppy seed heads, limonium, ammobium and love lies bleeding

- Thin wire such as bullion wire

- A vintage hair comb

I adore wearing flowers in my hair – I began creating these hair combs for brides, and now wear them myself too. They are the perfect alternative to glittery hair combs.

I source vintage hair combs from eBay and Etsy and keep my designs simple and carefree – but the possibilities of size and scale are endless for these. They're my grown-up version of the daisy chains I used to make and wear when I was young – less showy than a flower crown but with a nod to my love of nature.

LET'S GET STARTED

1. Lay your flowers and foliage out on a clean surface, stripping off any foliage you don't want and separating large blooms from smaller buds.

2. Take the wire and secure it to one end of the hair comb tucking in the loose end (see techniques, page 59).

3. Starting with a base of foliage, layer up one main stem of foliage, fanning out the others to the side with sprigs of seed heads and grasses. The way you position your materials will determine the shape and size of the hair comb, so consider where it will sit on your head and how big you want it to be before you start. For example, if you want a comb to sit on the side of your head, you might want to go for a slightly curved design that would follow the shape of your hair.

4. Start introducing your flowers, building them up slowly as you go. Consider different textures, and the depth of the material and continue to secure it by wrapping around and through the teeth of the hair comb with your wire as you go.

5. Once you've reached the end of your hair comb, you'll need to reverse the materials to complete the look. This can be super-fiddly when working with such small blooms and I find the best way is to create a small posy that is then laid with the bare stems sitting under the existing flowers.

6. To finish the hair comb, cut the wire from its reel and thread it through the underside loops of wire visible under the comb, as before, making sure the loose end is tucked safely out of the way to avoid it causing irritation when you wear it.

EXTRA

INSPIRATION

Try out flowers such as love lies bleeding, as they hang down beautifully.

Break off smaller flowers such as strawflowers for a less showy design.

Contrast the colour of the hair comb with the colour of the person's hair, to ensure it stands out.

DRIED FLOWER

B R A C E L E T

G A T H E R

- A selection of complementary dried material with solid stems – here I've used bracken and plum strawflowers, with bloom broom and ixodia supporting

- Florist wire

- A length of naturally dyed ribbon

This method is a really simple but effective way to wear dried flowers. A modern take on traditional corsages and accessible to us all.

LET'S GET STARTED

1. The structure of flowers for these
   bracelets follows a very similar pattern
   to the boutonnières on page 146. When
   bringing the elements together, check
   how they will sit on your wrist,
   tweaking as necessary.

2. Once you have your mini-posy
   constructed (see techniques, page 57),
   secure with florist wire, tucking the
   end in securely (see techniques, page
   59). Take your length of ribbon and at its
   central point, wrap it around the stalks –
   once should be enough, but if you have
   to you can wrap it around a few times.
   Tie in a knot at the back of the bouquet.
   This then sits on top of your wrist.

3. Place the bouquet in position on your
   wrist and tie the ribbon-ends in a double
   knot or a bow on your wrist's underside.
   Leave a length of ribbon to float around
   the wrist as an extra design touch.

4. Both the ribbon and the mini-posy
   can be reused once your event is over.
   The mini-posy can be used as a decoration
   in the house, either in a vase or on a
   mantlepiece or as a place setting (page 92).

EVERLASTING

BOUTONNIÈRE

GATHER

GATHER

- A selection of delicate blooms, seed heads and foliage with one statement flower – I've used honesty seed heads, bleached bloom broom, green phalaris and acrolinium flower

- Twine, string or raffia

- A dress pin

I could make these all day long! They're such a simple and easy creation – they look fabulous on a dark suit at a wedding or cute on a jacket for a summer party.

1. Start with your main flower – this will form the centre of your boutonnière. Build up the other flowers and materials around the main flower to form a sort of frame of smaller flowers around the central focal-point.

2. To secure the bunch in place, use florist wire (see techniques, page 59) and then take a length of beautiful string or twine and wrap it round the stalks of the bunch until they're completely covered, tying it in a very tight, neat, double knot at the back.

3. Trim the ends so they're neat and tidy, then secure them in place with the dress pin.

DRIED FLOWER

FLORAL CROWNS

GATHER

- Rustic wire

- A mix of complementary small-headed dried flowers – I used white acrolinium, statice sinuata, sanfordii, bloom broom and bupleurum

- Small meadow grasses such as quaking grass

- Small foliage leaves

- Bullion wire

- A length of naturally dyed silk ribbon

Crowns are the queen of floral wearables, and are usually worn on midsummer evening, at weddings, or at hen parties. They are divine in their subtlety, which makes them a strong choice of headwear for special occasions.

This method can be used to make fresh crowns as well as dried. Cornflowers, feverfew, buttercup and quaking grass work well and can also dry in place.

There are a few ways to make flower crowns; the method I use is layering the flowers on top of each other as I go – I prefer this to making lots of small bunches. It gives the flowers more freedom to move, resulting in a less-structured piece.

LET'S GET STARTED

1. Cut a length of your rustic wire, long enough to fit around your head, and turn both ends in to make small loops through which to loop your ribbon.

2. Prepare your dried materials by trimming the ends so they are roughly 5cm (2½ in) in length, and stripping off any unwanted leaves (see techniques, page 57).

3. Starting at one end of the rustic wire, tie the bullion wire to the flower crown wire base (see techniques, page 59).

4. Gather a pretty selection of your flowers and lay them over the top of your rustic wire – I prefer to introduce the main flower a little later on in the make. Wrap the bullion wire around the stalks of the flowers and seed heads a number of times to keep them in place. When wrapping the wire round, try to keep a little looseness in it to allow the flowers and foliage to move.

5. Continue to layer the flowers and foliage along the wire. Think about the structure and flow of the crown and, if you feel the need, take a look in the mirror with it held up to your head. How big and bold you go is up to you and the flowers you choose to use. For this crown, I selected very fine flowers for a delicate look.

6. Keep going until you're 5–10 cm (2–4 in) or so from the end and are ready to finish it off. Wrap the wire really tightly around the last stems, cutting off any unwanted lengths. Cover the exposed wire and stalks of the flowers by preparing a final posy of a selection of flowers that follow the existing structure of the flower crown. Lay this posy over the top of the final stalks, facing in the opposite direction.

7. Take the thin wire and wrap it around and under this posy. This can be a little fiddly, so take care – you're aiming to cover up all the stalks of the flowers going in both directions and also to make sure the crown flows all the way round.

8. Once you're sure the wire is holding the flowers in place securely, tuck the end of the wire through an existing loop to finish off and ensure that the end is not going to hurt your head when you put it on (see techniques, page 59).

9. Finish by looping your ribbon through both ends and tying it in a bow.

The crown can be hung on a bedroom wall or a vanity mirror as a display piece when you're not wearing it.

EXTRA

INSPIRATION

Celebrate midsummer eve by making a fresh flower crown with friends. Afterwards, hang the flower crown on your wall to dry.

For a less formal crown, use big and bold blooms in a smaller collection and sit to the side of your head.

AVAILABILITY OF MATERIAL

Whilst I am based in the UK and many of the flowers and foliage I speak of in this book are from the woods and hedgerows where I live, by searching for the Latin name of the flower (check out the growing pages 27–30) you'll be able to find an equivalent where you live. As I've mentioned in the book before, if you follow the principle of selecting more papery/woody stems and petals than fleshy/juicy, you'll have great success with drying! Of course, there are always anomalies - tulips and dahlias do dry beautifully!

SOURCING

If you are unable to grow your own or find a suitable place to forage then you can head to your local florist, flower market or flower farmer to source flowers for drying. As much as possible I try to stick with local suppliers for my makes, ensuring my blooms haven't travelled miles and miles to reach me.

WHEN THE END COMES

Even with the best love and care, there will come a time when you'll want to change up your dried flower displays for something fresher or perhaps more seasonal. Always aim to reuse your wreath-bases as much as possible and to compost any natural material so the goodness goes back into the earth.

CHEMICALS AND NASTIES

Trends come and go and at the time of writing this book, dyed and bleached flowers were becoming increasingly popular. Please consider the environment when investing in these flowers, the flowers go through an intense process full of chemicals to achieve this look which is not only damaging as a process but also means that these materials should not then be composted as those chemicals will go back into the earth. There are plenty of blooms out there that can give you the same muted soft tones.

DON'T WASTE A THING

If you decide to embark on creating after reading this book (I really hope you will!) then I urge you to make the most of all the materials you work with. Keep a box of dried flower heads for decorating gifts and place-settings with, make natural firelighters using old leaves, twigs and fircones.

A NOTE
ON DRIED
FLOWERS

To everyone who told me I could do it, who believed in me enough that my own self doubt began to crumble and to all those who asked me when I would be writing a book. Strangers, friends and family, small comments and emails scattered over the course of many years, taking me on this journey to writing Everlastings.

To Ed, for your patience and for your creative inputs. For helping me see the wood for the trees and for allowing me the time to write and think. For never giving up even when I shoot you down, you were often right and I know I struggled to admit that. Your support and encouragement is unfaltering and I could not have done this without you standing by my side cheering me on. To Henry and Arlo for opening my eyes to a different way of life and keeping me grounded by asking questions such as 'Is your book going to be any good mama?' and 'how bored are you of working on your book?'. You are my world and I am so grateful you played that day in the woods and wore my flower crowns with such grace and beauty, I love you all.

To my dear friend Lulu, a kindred spirit. I have so much to thank you for. Always ready to share your advice, you helped me in so many ways with this book. From reading my proposal to guiding me on who to work with and perhaps most importantly providing me with the best vintage wardrobe which is scattered through the pages.

And to Rachel, for producing the ethereal illustrations scattered through the book, I am so pleased you are part of this project, you've been on this journey with me since the very beginning.

A special thanks to my mum (ever the teacher) who proofread the document like an absolute pro and spotted so many things my eyes were too tired to see anymore.

To the wonderful community of growers and makers, who leaned in and shared their products and produce with me to feature in this book. You know who you are!

To Kajal, who saw the potential in my book proposal and never doubted that we would make something beautiful together. You have been a joy to work with and I am honoured to be part of the Hardie Grant family. To Eve and the project team behind the book, Polly, Matt and Jo – a perfect blend of creative, technical and emotional support across it all. Thank you for giving me so much freedom in my work. And to Claire Warner, whose design has brought to life the pages of the book in a way that is quite simply perfectly me.

To Laura, I can't thank you enough. You got me and my vision from day one and bought so much more to the table than I ever could have hoped for. Your talent knows no bounds and you're also an awesome human being, thank you.

THANKS

INDEX

One of the things I love the most about what I do is the connections I make with other suppliers. Whether that be local flower farmers down the road from me or a maker of naturally dyed materials, all these people make up the fabric of a business. Here are a few of my favourite suppliers:

THE NATURAL DYE WORKS

Ros creates the most wonderful naturally dyed fabrics from her home in Kent.
thenaturaldyeworks.com

LOCAL FLOWER FARMERS

As much as possible I buy locally and I would urge you to find your own local supplier of flowers.

www.flowersfromthefarm.co.uk is a good place to start.

DRIED FLOWER FARMERS

Here are a few online places to source dried flowers from. But, do also consider local flower farmers who are moving into offering dried flowers in the autumn and winter.

Essentially Hops: www.essentiallyhops.co.uk
Just Dhalias: www.justdhalias.co.uk
Atlas Flowers: www.atlasflowers.com

WORKSHOP LTD

Nadine creates beautiful homewares and is the maker behind my brilliant brass hoops.
workshop.ltd

ROWEN & WREN

An online store with a perfectly curated collection of home and garden ware.
rowenandwren.co.uk

KHADI PAPERS

For handmade 100 per cent natural papers to create cards from.
khadi.com

HAMPSHIRE HOPS

This local business sell hop vines as well as hop pines – so naked or with the flowers! My favourite wreath base to work with.
instagram.com/hampshirehops

Everlastings by Bex Partridge

ISBN: 978-1-78488-339-3
10 9 8 7 6 5

Publishing Director: Kate Pollard
Commissioning Editor: Kajal Mistry
Senior Editor: Eve Marleau
Design: Claire Warner Studio
Illustration: Rachel Thomas Jones
Photography: Laura Edwards
Photography Assistants:
Jo Cowan, Matthew Hague
Prop styling: Polly Webb-Wilson
Copy-editor: Gregor Shepherd
Proofreader: Taahir Husain
Indexer: Vanessa Bird

Colour Reproduction by p2d
Printed and bound in China
by Leo Paper Products Ltd

Published in 2020 by Hardie Grant Books,
an imprint of Hardie Grant Publishing

Hardie Grant Books (London)
5th & 6th Floors
52–54 Southwark Street
London SE1 1UN

Hardie Grant Books (Melbourne)
Building 1, 658 Church Street
Richmond, Victoria 3121

hardiegrantbooks.com

Copyright text © Bex Partridge 2020

Copyright photography © Laura Edwards 2020

British Library Cataloguing-in-Publication
Data. A catalogue record for this book is
available from the British Library.